THE HISTORY OF THE KANSAS CITY CHIEFS

Published by Creative Education

123 South Broad Street

Mankato, Minnesota 56001

Creative Education is an imprint of The Creative Company.

DESIGN AND PRODUCTION BY **EVANSDAY DESIGN**

LIBRARY OF CONGRESS CATALOGING-IN-PUBLICATION DATA

Hawkes, Brian (Brian F.)

The history of the Kansas City Chiefs / by Brian Hawkes.

p. cm. — (NFL today)

Summary: Traces the history of the team from its beginnings through 2003.

ISBN 1-58341-301-4

1. Kansas City Chiefs (Football team)—History—Juvenile literature.

[1. Kansas City Chiefs (Football team)—History. 2. Football—History.]

I. Title. II. Series.

GV956.K35H39 2004

796.332'64'09778411—dc22   2003062578

First edition

9 8 7 6 5 4 3 2 1

COVER PHOTO: running back Priest Holmes

PHOTOGRAPHS BY

AP/Wide World Photos, Corbis (Bettmann, UPI/Corbis-Bettmann), Getty Images, SportsChrome USA

THERE ARE TWO **KANSAS CITIES** LOCATED IN THE CENTRAL UNITED STATES, SEPARATED BY THE MISSOURI RIVER. KANSAS CITY, MISSOURI, IS LOCATED ALONG THE WESTERN EDGE OF THE STATE, WHILE KANSAS CITY, KANSAS, IS AT THE EASTERN EDGE OF THAT STATE. KANSAS CITY, MISSOURI, THE LARGER OF THE NEIGHBORING "TWIN" CITIES, IS A BUSTLING METROPOLITAN AREA THAT IS HOME TO MORE THAN 500,000 PEOPLE. NEXT TO ST. LOUIS, IT IS THE LARGEST CITY IN MISSOURI.

LONG BEFORE THE CITIES OF KANSAS CITY AND ST. LOUIS WERE FOUNDED, NATIVE AMERICAN TRIBES FLOURISHED ON THE PLAINS OF MISSOURI. SO WHEN A NATIONAL FOOTBALL LEAGUE (NFL) TEAM SETTLED IN KANSAS CITY IN 1963, IT WAS NAMED THE KANSAS CITY CHIEFS. SINCE THAT START MORE THAN 40 YEARS AGO, THE CHIEFS HAVE BEEN SHOWING FANS IN THE "SHOW ME" STATE OF MISSOURI AN EXCITING BRAND OF FOOTBALL

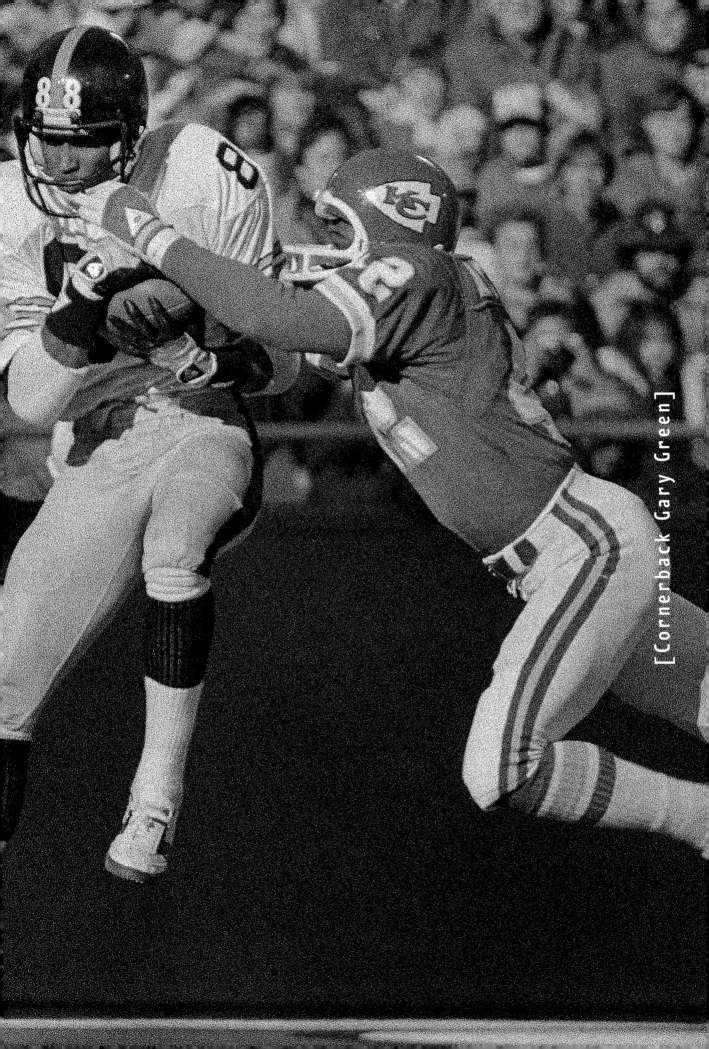

[Cornerback Gary Green]

A PLACE TO CALL HOME>

THE CHIEFS ACTUALLY started out not in Missouri, but on the plains of Texas as a team called the Dallas Texans. In 1960, the Texans became one of the original eight teams in a professional league called the American Football League (AFL). The owner of the Texans, Lamar Hunt, was a native Texan who wanted his team to thrive in his home state. But later in 1960, an expansion team for the older, more established NFL came to town—the Dallas Cowboys. In their first two seasons, the Texans went a combined 14–14 and had trouble drawing fans.

In 1962, the Texans' first coach, Hank Stram, added former NFL quarterback Len Dawson to the team. Dawson had struggled with the Pittsburgh Steelers and Cleveland Browns, but Coach Stram believed he had the potential to become a top-notch passer. After working to refine his throwing technique, Dawson led the surprising Texans to an 11–3 record and the AFL Western Division title in 1962.

Dawson didn't do it all by himself, though. Elusive running back Abner Haynes scored a league-record 19 touchdowns that season, and linebacker Sherrill Headrick and cornerback Dave Grayson spearheaded a fierce defense. In the 1962 AFL championship game, these players carried the Texans to a 20–17 overtime victory over their intrastate rivals, the Houston Oilers.

Despite capturing the AFL championship, the Texans still struggled to sell tickets, as most Dallas fans gave their support to the NFL's Cowboys. Hunt finally decided to move his team, and before the 1963 season, the Texans relocated to Kansas City and became known as the Kansas City Chiefs. Although the great play of Dawson and Haynes quickly won over Kansas City fans, the Chiefs were a mediocre team in their first two seasons.

K.C. ON THE WARPATH>

IN 1965, THE Chiefs added another offensive weapon by drafting a 6-foot-3 and 215-pound receiver named Otis Taylor. The young receiver had it all: size, speed, strength, and agility. He also had confidence. "I'll tell you something about Otis Taylor," he said. "He wants to be the best—always. There hasn't been a year when he didn't want to score more touchdowns than anybody and gain more yardage than anybody. At the start of the season, I aim for the top 10 and higher. And I don't quit."

In 1965, Taylor helped the Chiefs go 7–5–2. By 1966, Kansas City was poised for another run at a championship. Such talented additions as linebackers Bobby Bell and E.J. Holub helped the team put together an 11–2–1 record and win the Western Division. The Chiefs then pounded the Buffalo Bills, 31–7, to bring home the franchise's second AFL title.

In previous years, winning the AFL championship would have been the ultimate accomplishment. But in 1966, the AFL champs were to take on the NFL champs to determine a true world champion. The game was to be called the AFL-NFL World Championship Game. Lamar Hunt didn't like the name. "Why don't we just call it the Super Bowl?" he suggested. It was a name that would stick. Super Bowl I pitted the Chiefs against the heavily favored NFL champion Green Bay Packers.

More than 65 million people tuned in their television sets to watch the first Super Bowl. After Green Bay struck first, Dawson threw a touchdown pass to fullback Curtis McClinton to tie the game in the second quarter. But the Packers and their star quarterback, Bart Starr, proved too powerful for the Chiefs, pulling away in the second half to win 35–10.

HAIL TO THE CHIEFS>

IN 1968, THE Chiefs went 12–2 and returned to the playoffs, only to lose to the Oakland Raiders. But in 1969, the Chiefs made a triumphant return to the Super Bowl. Behind a hard-hitting defense that featured such stars as linebacker Willie Lanier and tackle Buck Buchanan, Kansas City went 11–3. The team then beat the New York Jets and Oakland Raiders to advance to the Super Bowl, where it faced the NFL champion Minnesota Vikings.

Even though the AFL's New York Jets had won Super Bowl III in a stunning 16–7 upset over the NFL's mighty Baltimore Colts, most football fans called it a fluke. The NFL was still seen as superior to the AFL, and oddsmakers made the Vikings 13-point favorites to win the Super Bowl. After all, Kansas City had lost by a wide margin in the first Super Bowl. The Chiefs were not worried, though; they knew that this was a different Kansas City team.

Kicker Jan Stenerud booted three field goals to give the Chiefs an early 9–0 lead over the Vikings. Then, with the score 16–7, Dawson hit Taylor with a short pass. The star receiver scampered 46 yards for a touchdown, sealing a 23–7 Chiefs victory. "Our game plan wasn't very complicated," a joyful Dawson explained after the game. "It involved throwing a lot of formations at them—formations they hadn't seen during the course of the season."

The Chiefs remained a strong team over the next few seasons but could not make it back to the Super Bowl, despite some great performances by scrappy halfback Ed Podolak. In 1970, the AFL merged with the NFL, and a year later the Chiefs met the Miami Dolphins in the NFL playoffs. At the end of regulation, the score was tied 24–24. The game went into overtime…and then a second overtime. Finally, the Dolphins kicked a field goal to hand the Chiefs a 27–24 loss. That 82-minute contest still stands as the longest NFL game in history.

In 1972, the Chiefs moved into Arrowhead Stadium, a beautiful new stadium with almost 80,000 seats. The team struggled during the first two seasons in its new home, missing the playoffs both times. Still, faithful Chiefs fans filled up the stadium to cheer for such great players as Pro Bowl cornerback Emmitt Thomas and linebacker Bobby Bell.

THE LATE 1970S were difficult seasons in Kansas City. Head coach Hank Stram was fired after the 1974 season, and Dawson and Taylor retired a year later. Without these leaders, the Chiefs slipped to last place. New heroes emerged, including defensive end Art Still, but Kansas City remained at the bottom of the American Football Conference (AFC) Western Division standings the rest of the decade.

Under new coach Marv Levy, the Chiefs climbed to a respectable 8–8 in 1980. The team's future looked bright in 1981, when the Chiefs drafted running back Joe Delaney. Delaney stood only 5-foot-9 and weighed just 185 pounds, but he made up for it with quick feet and a big heart.

In his rookie season, Delaney rushed for 1,121 yards and was named the AFC Rookie of the Year. And with a solid defense led by Still and safety Gary Barbaro, the Chiefs finished the season 9–7.

Then, just as the team was moving up, tragedy struck. On June 29, 1983, in an act of heroic courage, Delaney died while trying to save three boys who were drowning in a lake. Delaney's college coach, A.L. Williams, said, "People ask me, 'How could Joe have gone in the water the way he did?' And I answer, 'Why, he never gave it a second thought, because helping people was a conditioned reflex to Joe Delaney.'"

Still reeling from the death of their young star, the Chiefs slipped to 6–10 in 1983. It wasn't until 1986 that the Chiefs broke their decade-long drought and made the playoffs. Unfortunately, the Chiefs' playoff run was a short one, as they lost to the New York Jets in the first round.

PLAYOFF STREAKING IN THE '90s>

IN THE LATE 1980s, Kansas City used the NFL Draft

to stockpile new talent. In 1987, the Chiefs drafted

Christian Okoye, a gigantic (6-foot-3 and 260 pounds)

running back known for his battering-ram rushing style.

The "Nigerian Nightmare," as he was nicknamed, would

lead the team in rushing four times, including a club-

record 1,480-yard season in 1989. The team also drafted

such outstanding defenders as end Neil Smith, linebacker

Derrick Thomas, and cornerback Dale Carter. This trio an-

chored a defense that emerged as one of the NFL's best

in the early 1990s.

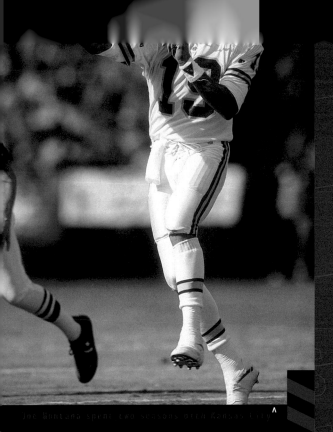

Joe Montana spent two seasons with Kansas City ^

The Chiefs made the playoffs every year from 1990 to 1995. In 1991, they earned their first playoff victory in 22 years, beating the Los Angeles Raiders 10–6. One of the key reasons for the Chiefs' turnaround was the greater sense of confidence instilled by their new coach, Marty Schottenheimer. "The best way to establish a position of excellence in the NFL," Schottenheimer explained, "is to expect it."

After the chiefs made a quick playoff exit in 1992, Coach Schottenheimer made a major move by bringing in two Hall of Fame veterans: legendary quarterback Joe Montana and running back Marcus Allen. With these veterans added to the team's youthful lineup, the Chiefs went 11–5 in 1993, then charged all the way to the AFC championship game. Unfortunately, they fell just short of the Super Bowl, losing to the Buffalo Bills 30–13.

The Chiefs seemed even stronger two seasons later, going 13–3 in 1995 before being upset in the playoffs by the Indianapolis Colts. That turned out to be the Chiefs' last best chance at a championship in the '90s. The team made the playoffs once more in 1997 with the help of such players as receiver Andre Rison and guard Will Shields, but lost 14–10 to the Denver Broncos. After that, the Chiefs slipped from the top of the AFC West.

A CHIEFS UPRISING>

ALTHOUGH THE CHIEFS remained a losing team in 2000, there were reasons for optimism in Kansas City. One of these reasons was tight end Tony Gonzalez. That season, the 6-foot-4 and 250-pound end—who had also been an outstanding basketball player during his college career at the University of California—caught an incredible 93 passes for 1,203 yards.

In 2001, Gonzalez was joined by a new coach and two new offensive leaders. The new coach was Dick Vermeil, who had led the St. Louis Rams to a Super Bowl victory just two years earlier. The two new offensive leaders were quarterback Trent Green and explosive running back Priest Holmes. The team's defense, meanwhile, was sparked by linebacker Donnie Edwards.

Kansas City went a combined 14–18 in 2001 and 2002, but its high-powered offense began to open eyes around the league. In 2001, Green passed for 3,783 yards, and Gonzalez posted nearly 1,000 receiving yards again. In 2002, the spotlight

Donnie Edwards led the team in tackles for four years.

was squarely on Holmes. In the finest season of his career, the quick but powerful halfback broke loose for an AFC-best 1,615 yards and scored a whopping 24 touchdowns. "He is doing stuff that has never been done in the history of the NFL, especially with those touchdowns," Gonzalez said of the electrifying Holmes. "It's getting out of control."

In 2003, the high-powered Chiefs raced to a stunning 9–0 start before finishing the season 13–3. Holmes scored an NFL-record 27 touchdowns on the season, while spectacular kick returner Dante Hall made history of his own by running a kick back for a touchdown in four straight games. Unfortunately, the Chiefs' defense was not nearly as strong as their offense, and the team fell to the Indianapolis Colts in the playoffs, 38–31.

For more than four decades, fans in the "Show Me" state have cheered for the team with the arrowhead on its helmet. From an appearance in the first-ever Super Bowl, to a Super Bowl victory in 1969, to six consecutive playoff berths in the 1990s, the Kansas City Chiefs have been counted among the NFL's elite more often than not. As today's Chiefs continue down the warpath, they intend to bring another NFL championship to western Missouri very soon.

INDEX>